Genre Realistic

 Essential Question
How do animals survive?

Where Are They Going?

by Brian Hannigan

illustrated by Ana Ocha

Chapter I
A New Noise 2

Chapter 2
Flying South 5

Chapter 3
Lots of Birds 9

Chapter 4
Time Flies, Too I4

Respond to Reading I6

PAIRED READ A Whale's Journey I7

Focus on Genre 20

Chapter 1
A New Noise

Grandpa and Emma stood outside.

Grandpa said, "What a beautiful day! I love to smell the fresh country air."

Emma did not say anything, and she did not smile. She was unhappy.

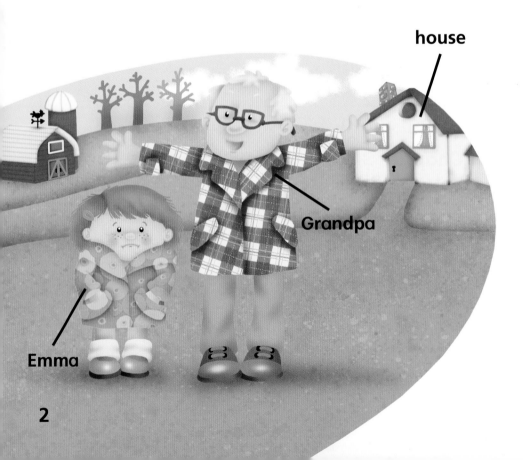

house

Grandpa

Emma

Emma said, "It is so quiet here. The silence is strange. In the city, I hear noise all the time."

Emma did not tell Grandpa, but she felt a little homesick. She missed the city and her parents.

flock

Suddenly, Emma heard a sound. She asked, "What is that honking noise? I don't see any cars."

Grandpa pointed to the sky. Emma looked up and saw a big V shape.

Grandpa said, "It is a flock of birds called snow geese."

STOP AND CHECK

What does Emma hear and see?

4

Chapter 2
Flying South

geese

Emma asked, "Where are the birds going?"

Grandpa said, "They are flying south. They live in the north, but the climate is too cold in the winter. So the birds adapt. They fly to a warm area and stay for the winter. Then they return home in the spring."

Emma watched the birds fly away.
She thought, *I wish I had freedom
like that. Then I could fly back to
my house.*

Emma pulled her jacket tighter.
She tried not to think about home.

jacket

Then Emma heard more honking. She looked and saw another V of geese.

Emma asked, "How do the geese know where to go? Do they have a good sense of direction?"

Grandpa said, "I don't know. Would you like to find out?"

"Yes," Emma said.

Grandpa said, "Then let's go inside!"

> **In Other Words**   learn about it.
> En español: *averiguar.*

STOP AND CHECK

What does Emma want to find out?

8

Chapter 3
Lots of Birds

table

Emma and Grandpa went into the kitchen.

Grandma put out tea, mugs, and fruit.

Emma said, "We saw snow geese! I want to find out about them."

couch

"That is a wonderful idea," Grandma said. "We can look at bird books, magazines, and the computer."

Language Detective This sentence includes commas (,) to show a series of things. Find commas in a series on page 9.

Grandma got two bird books and gave one to Emma.

Emma found the chapter on *snow goose* in the book. She read, *"Snow geese migrate in huge flocks. Some flocks have 1,000 birds.* That is why they are so loud."

book

Snow Goose

Grandma read from her book. She said, "Snow geese can fly about 40 miles an hour. That is as fast as a car!"

Emma said, "The geese fly thousands of miles. They fly day and night!"

Emma closed her book and went to look on the computer.

chair

computer

Emma read that baby snow geese fly south with their parents.

Emma said, "Scientists think the baby geese learn how to migrate. They learn how to get to the winter nesting grounds. Then they learn how to fly home."

STOP AND CHECK

What did Emma learn about snow geese?

13

Chapter 4
Time Flies, Too

Emma kept reading. Then Grandma said, "It's time to make dinner!"

Emma said, "So soon? I did not think it was that late."

Grandma said, "Time flies just like the birds!" Emma laughed.

In Other Words time goes by quickly. En español: *el tiempo vuela.*

bed

That night, Emma lay in bed. She looked at the shadows on the wall. The shadows looked like flying geese.

Emma thought, *I had fun today.* She was eager to have more fun tomorrow.

Then Emma fell asleep. She dreamed she was flying.

STOP AND CHECK

How does Emma feel now?

Summarize

Use important details to summarize *Where Are They Going?*

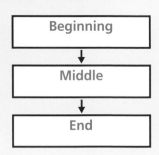

Beginning

Middle

End

Text Evidence

1. How do you know that *Where Are They Going* is realistic fiction? Genre

2. Who are the characters in the story? What do they do? Use story details to support your answer. Plot

3. Use what you know about prefixes to figure out the meaning of the word *unhappy* on page 2. Prefixes

4. Write about how Emma changes in this story. Use story details to support your answer. Write About Reading

Compare Texts
Read about another animal that migrates.

A Whale's Journey

Humpback whales are huge animals. They can be up to fifty feet long! How is a humpback like a bird? Both animals migrate.

A humpback whale is big and strong.

Humpbacks adapt to changes in the water around them.

The whales live near Alaska. The water is cold in the summer. It is filled with food.

The water is too cold in the winter. The whales swim to warmer waters.

Many humpback whales swim to Hawaii in winter.

snow

water

This baby humpback will stay with its mother.

Baby whales are born in the warm waters. They swim north with their mothers in the summer.

Make Connections

How do humpback whales survive?
Essential Question

How are humpback whales and snow geese alike? Text to Text

Focus on
Genre

Realistic Fiction Realistic fiction is a made-up story. But it could happen in real life. The people and places are like real people and places.

What to Look For Emma and her grandparents in *Where Are They Going?* are like real people. The story happens on a farm. This place seems real. The story events could happen in real life.

Your Turn

Plan a realistic fiction story. Make a story map. Include the characters, setting, and plot. Be sure the people, places, and events could be real. Tell what happens in the beginning, middle, and end of your story.